BITCOIN

Mark Edwards

THE ULTIMATE POCKET GUIDE FOR BEGINNERS IN BITCOIN AND CRYPTOCURRENCY WORLD

MARK EDWARDS

Bitcoin : The Ultimate Pocket Guide for Beginners in Bitcoin and Cryptocurrency World

UUID: 67d96188-1431-11e8-9a22-17532927e555

Ce livre a été créé avec StreetLib Write
(http://write.streetlib.com).

ISBN : 978-0-244-96930-1

table des matières

BITCOIN

The Ultimate Pocket Guide for Beginners in Bitcoin and Cryptocurrency World

Bitcoin :
The Ultimate Pocket Guide for Beginners in Bitcoin
and Cryptocurrency World

BITCOIN

The Ultimate Pocket Guide for Beginners in Bitcoin and Cryptocurrency World

Bitcoin: The Ultimate Pocket Guide for Beginners in Cryptocurrency World

STRATEGIES FOR BITCOIN AND CRYPTOCURRENCY INVESTORS

Investing in highly volatile bitcoins and other cryptocurrencies is risky business. These currencies are all electronic or virtual in nature, and thus have no physical presence. They don't even have intrinsic value. However, no one can deny that right now these cryptocurrencies are extremely valuable and those who invested in the early days, and held on to their investments, are living the high life now as multi-millionaires, and even billionaires!

If you want to be like these wise investors sometime in the future, then follow these 4 investing strategies to increase your chances for success.

1 - PREPARE FOR VOLATILITY

It's basically a given for cryptocurrencies that they are going to be extremely volatile. One minute the price is sitting at 5 digits, and the next it's at 4 or even 3 digits! It's absolutely unpredictable, and if you don't take its volatility seriously, you could get in a lot of trouble. You could panic and sell off your crypto so you can minimize your loss.

However, if you've braced yourself for scenarios like this, then you'd probably just shut down your computer, or turn off your TV, and lie down and sleep off your doubts. Tomorrow is a different day, the price could go back up, and all will be fine with the world. Being prepared for volatility is tough, but it's definitely doable.

2 - PROCEED WITH CAUTION

Do your research before you start investing in bitcoins and other cryptocurrencies. When you're dealing with hard-earned money, you don't want to lose everything in one day. You're investing to make a profit sometime in the future. Don't go all in without studying what you're putting your money into.

3 - DIVERSIFY YOUR PORTFOLIO

Don't put all your eggs in one basket, so to speak. Don't just invest in bitcoins. If possible, invest in other crypto-currencies as well as traditional assets like stocks, bonds, and mutual funds. At least if bitcoin prices drop, then you're not going to be totally in the red. Your other investments will help keep you afloat.

4 - STORE YOUR VIRTUAL COINS IN COLD WALLETS

Investing is a long-term game, and it is not advisable to keep your cryptocurrencies in online wallets such as your exchange's wallet, or even your mobile app wallet. Keep your private keys in cold wallets such as paper or hardware wallets since these aren't connected to the Internet. You can keep small amounts in your online wallets, but the bulk of your investments should be offline.

5 INTERESTING FACTS ABOUT BLOCKCHAIN TECHNOLOGY

Blockchain is the technology that makes Bitcoin and other cryptocurrencies very secure. It's an open-source and distributed database that is stored in nodes or computers within the network. When new transactions or blocks are added to the blockchain, it will automatically update itself. Here are 5 very interesting facts about this ultra-modern technology.

1 – IT'S TAMPER-PROOF

Once an entry has been added onto the blockchain, it will be nearly impossible to remove or alter it later. If you want to alter an entry, you'd have to basically alter all the transactions that came after it. Doing this is mathematically impossible, so even genius fraudsters would have to look elsewhere to steal bitcoins without too much effort. Being tamper-proof is also the reason bitcoin payments are final and irreversible.

2 – IT'S 100% TRANSPARENT

Anyone with access to the blockchain can see all the transactions that have ever occurred in the past. You can even look up the first ever block (block 0) that was mined by Bitcoin founder, Satoshi Nakamoto, in 2009. This genesis block contained the message " *T h e Times 03/Jan/2009 Chancellor on brink of second bailout for banks.* "

3 – CRIMINALS CAN'T HIDE BEHIND THE BLOCKCHAIN

If criminals think they can hide behind the relative anonymity that Bitcoin provides, they're sorely mistaken. Many have tried to evade the long arm of the law by converting their stolen loot to bitcoins and transferring them to different wallets, but with the transparent nature of the blockchain, computer experts can spot and trace all the bitcoin transactions these criminals have ever done.

4 - BLOCKCHAIN TECHNOLOGY IS NOT LIMITED TO CRYPTOCURREN-CIES

Many different startups have started to experiment with implementing blockchain technology in various industries. Once such example is Ethereum with their smart contracts technology which basically runs on blockchain. Since the blockchain is decentralized, two parties can make transactions between themselves without needing the services of a middleman. This not only saves you money, but it also saves you a lot of time and conflict.

5 – BLOCKCHAIN CAN STILL BE IMPROVED

While this technology has definitely improved the lives of many people, it can still be improved. For one, as time passes by, the blockchain will grow to be several hundred gigabytes of data. This will cause a lot of bandwidth and storage problems on personal computers. Let's hope the brightest minds in the crypto space can find a solution to this predicament soon.

AN ELEMENTARY EXPLANATION OF HOW BITCOIN WORKS

To most people, Bitcoin can seem like a financial concept made in a parallel universe. Yes, it's a very complex and complicated concept, but it doesn't mean it's impossible to learn it. When you think about it, many people started off with no idea about bitcoins and how it worked. But look at them now, they're probably investing left and right in various cryptocurrencies like pros and possibly profiting very nicely as well! So, in this article, we'll try to simplify how Bitcoin works using a betting game analogy:

Imagine playing a betting game with your friends, but none of you have any money on hand, so you decide to use a ledger to record the transactions, like your winnings and losses. But you don't want to put your trust on one friend to record everything, so a lot of you decide to make a ledger simultaneously.

This way, at the end of each game, those who kept ledgers can compare their records to see if it all evens out—which means that cheating the system would be virtually impossible unless everybody else is in cahoots with you, which ultimately defeats the purpose of cheating in the first place.

The ledger is not hidden or exclusive to the ledger keepers; you can view it anytime you want. To add your transactions to the ledger, all you have to do is broadcast your transactions to the ledger keepers, and you pay as little or as much as you want to make sure they put your name down on that ledger as soon as possible.

Your friends who keep the ledgers up to date get compensation for their hard work with a reward in the form of money. This money comes from an external source—say, a vault with a limited amount of money. The money in the vault wasn't part of the money circulating in the betting pool, but it became so once it was acquired by your ledger-keeper friends.

This simple analogy is exactly how Bitcoin operates, albeit on a much more complicated level. Bitcoin runs on a global computer network, and each transaction is compiled into new blocks which are then connected to the last block on the blockchain. And the bitcoin miners are the ledger-keepers who work hard to record transactions and mine those precious bitcoins.

BITCOIN IS THE FUTURE OF MONEY IN DEVELOPING ECONOMIES

Bitcoin is fast becoming integrated into the everyday lives of people living in developing countries. With unstable and hyper-inflated national currencies, bitcoins are proving to be a much more viable solution to solving the financial woes of their citizens. Here are 4 reasons why Bitcoin has a massive appeal for the masses in developing countries:

1 – YOU DON'T NEED BANKS

In developed countries, it's relatively easy to sign up for bank accounts and credit cards. But in the developing world, it's a vastly different story. It's much harder to get credit and setting up a bank account is no walk in the park. But Bitcoin changes all that. With Bitcoin, you can save your own bitcoins yourself – all you need is a secure wallet to keep your digital money safe.

2 – FAST, CHEAP AND BORDERLESS PAYMENTS

With Bitcoin, you can send any amount of bitcoin to anyone in the world in a matter of minutes. When you send money through banks you not only pay those costly bank fees, you also need to wait for several hours or a few banking days. But with Bitcoin, as we've mentioned previously, you don't need banks to send or remit payments to other people. All you need is their bitcoin address and voila! Your payment should arrive in the next 10 or so minutes.

3 – BITCOIN CAN'T BE MANIPULATED BY ANYONE

Governments and banks can dictate the production and movement of their national currencies which ultimately leads to inflation. Unlike fiat currency, however, Bitcoin is a decentralized virtual currency. This means there is no controlling entity that tells the Bitcoin network what to do. Everything has been hard-coded into the network and the underlying technology behind Bitcoin, the blockchain, is tamper-proof and can't be manipulated by anyone, not even its developer, Satoshi Nakamoto.

4 – BITCOIN WILL HELP AUTHORITIES CATCH CRIMINALS

Contrary to popular belief, Bitcoin is not anonymous. Rather, it is a pseudonymous currency because while your alphanumeric public keys provide a certain level of anonymity, computer experts can trace who owns which wallets and the amount of bitcoins each wallet contains. Now the masses who make small transactions don't have anything to worry about. It's the criminals who move large amounts of bitcoins that catch authorities' attention, and it's who they focus their research on, not the millions of people who make minute transactions.

GETTING PAID IN BITCOIN FOR YOUR SERVICES – IS IT WORTH IT?

Before Bitcoin prices reached 5 digits, many people, freelancers mostly, were already getting paid in bitcoin. But now that prices have reached all-time highs, people are thinking of joining the fray and getting paid for their services or products, not in fiat currency, but in bitcoins. The big question is, is it worth it?

Some may say it's not worth it because bitcoin is extremely volatile. One minute the price is at a certain amount and the next 5 minutes, it's down by several hundred dollars. If you've put a lot of effort into your work, then you might feel faint at the thought of losing your hard-earned cash in a matter of minutes. Of course, this scenario will only happen if you decide to hold on to your bitcoins instead of exchanging it for your local currency at your favorite cryptocurrency exchange.

Imagine this second scenario though: what if you held on to your bitcoins and the price suddenly jumped to twice the original price? Then you'd feel like you've won the jackpot, right? Because you're essentially going to get paid at twice your rate! If the bitcoin you've received is equivalent to, say, for example, your salary of $5,000, with bitcoin prices going up twice the original amount, then you just got paid $10,000! That's pretty exciting, to say the least.

The decision to get paid in bitcoin is, of course, yours alone. But there are so many positive benefits to this cryptocurrency you should at least look at the bright side before you say no to an employer or client who's thinking of switching you over to bitcoin payments.

Bitcoin payments are fast and cheap. You no longer have to wait days for payment to arrive at your bank and you don't need to pay those hefty bank fees your bank charges you for withdrawing your money. You can receive bitcoin payments any time of the day, and you'll usually receive it within 10-45 minutes.

If you're averse to the volatility of bitcoin, you might want to consider holding a very small part, maybe 5% to 10% of the total amount, and exchanging the rest to your local currency. Who knows, you just might be able to take advantage of Bitcoin's volatility and before you know it, your bitcoins might be worth more than your entire year's salary.

KEEPING YOUR BITCOINS SAFE: HOT WALLETS VS. COLD WALLETS

There are basically two general types of wallets to keep your bitcoins, and other cryptocurrencies, safe. There are cold wallets and hot wallets. In this article, you'll find out the pros and cons of each type of wallet so you can make an informed decision when choosing which wallet to go for.

HOT WALLETS

Hot wallets are called hot because they are connected to the Internet which generally means it's easier for hackers to hack into and steal your valuable coins from you. Examples of hot wallets include those free wallets at your favorite bitcoin exchange website like Coinbase or Kraken, and mobile app wallets.

Desktop wallets are another form of hot wallets especially if you install it on a system that's connected to the Internet. However, you do have control over your private keys, and you can encrypt your wallet to prevent hacking attempts. The only downside to desktop wallets is if your computer gets destroyed or stolen, then you can pretty much say goodbye to your bitcoins.

There have been many instances of theft in hot wallets. Some hackers have even managed to steal millions of dollars' worth of bitcoins! Hot wallets are great for storing small amounts and transacting on the fly. But if you've got quite a sizeable number of bitcoins, then it's best to move these to offline storage or cold wallets.

COLD WALLETS

Cold wallets are the preferred storage method of people with a significant amount of bitcoins. Examples of cold wallet include paper wallets and hardware wallets. Paper wallets may sound a bit funny at first because we're talking about storing digital currencies here, but it's precisely why it's one of the best types of wallet for long-term storage! With paper wallets, there is zero chance of anyone hacking anything on paper. The downside is it can be stolen, or it can get burned, or destroyed. To keep your paper wallet safe, consider putting it in a safe environment like a safety deposit box.

The second type of cold wallet is the hardware wallet. It's a physical offline device that's pretty much like a glorified USB that can be plugged into your computer when you need to make a transaction. There are three main brands that are very popular among crypto owners. These are Trezor, Ledger Nano, and KeepKey. All three will cost you some money but will definitely help keep your virtual treasure chest safe.

SHOULD YOU TRADE OR INVEST IN BITCOINS?

Trading and investing may sound the same, but in reality, they are as different as day and night. Trading refers to a short-term method of trying to profit from buying and selling of bitcoins while investing refers to a long-term strategy where a buyer will hold on to their bitcoins for a long time and ride out any dips in the market price.

THE BITCOIN TRADER

The Bitcoin trader thrives on the exciting volatility of bitcoins. They'll try to time the market and buy bitcoins when the price dips and then they'll wait for the price to go up before they sell their bitcoins. Trading is a high-risk game because you're betting for the price to go up or down. Not everyone can trade, however. The most successful traders are those who have nerves of steel and can detach their emotions from their trades.

Traders don't get scared of dips in the price because they are optimistic it's going to go up again, sooner or later. They are looking to maximize their profits, too, so they'll mostly invest a lump sum and buy at the lowest price they can possibly go for, and then they'll wait until the price is high enough for them to make significant profit.

Trading takes a lot of guts. It takes a lot of thought and analysis. If you're an emotional type of person who gets physically sick with every dip in bitcoin price, then you're better off investing, and not trading, in bitcoins.

THE BITCOIN INVESTOR

Bitcoin investors are different from traders. They're in it for the long haul. They're not looking to take advantage of short-term fluctuations in the exchange rate. If the price goes down by hundreds or thousands of dollars, they're probably going to get worried, but they're not going to pull out their investment because they've already decided they're going to hold it for the next 10, 20 or 30 years.

A wise investor will practice the dollar cost averaging method to manage risk. This means whether the price goes up or down, they're going to buy bitcoins and hold them. This strategy is perfect for long-term investments as you're essentially spreading the risk. Though profits may not be as significant as short-term trading, the bitcoin investor probably sleeps easier at night as they're not worried how the charts are going to look like tomorrow or the day after.

THE 5 ADVANTAGES BITCOIN HAS OVER FIAT CURRENCY

Bitcoin is the first successful cryptocurrency in history, and it became successful because of the many positive merits not found in traditional or fiat currency (this is your country's national currency). In this article, you'll find out about five advantages Bitcoin has over fiat currency.

1 - BITCOIN IS DECENTRALIZED

Unlike fiat currency, Bitcoin is not controlled by any bank or government. No single entity controls or regulates the Bitcoin network, not even its founder Satoshi Nakamoto. Without a controlling entity, bitcoins are technically inflation-proof since no one can devalue its price by manipulating its supply. Only 21 million bitcoins will ever be mined or created, unlike fiat currency which is printed when the government sees fit to print more money.

2 – EXTREMELY EASY TO USE

Opening bank accounts is not a simple thing to do. You'd have to go to your bank, wait in line, fill out forms, submit your IDs, etc. It's a time-consuming process. But with Bitcoin, all you need to do to get started is just create a free wallet, and that's it! You'll then be able to receive your first bitcoins in just a few minutes.

3 - FAST TRANSACTIONS

Most banks don't work 24/7. Instead, banks are open for business during certain hours of the day on weekdays (some banks are open on weekends, but they're far and few in between). But with Bitcoin, you can transact with anyone, any time of the day, wherever you and the other person may be located. Your bitcoins will arrive in just a few minutes.

4 – HIGHLY PORTABLE AND DURA-BLE

Since bitcoins are electronic, they can't get burned down by fire, and they're not going to get wet in water. You can bring them anywhere with you, and they won't even take too much space. Whether you have an online wallet, or an offline wallet, your bitcoins are easily within reach anytime you wish.

5 - NO MORE EXORBITANT BANK FEES

Bank fees are the bane of anyone who has ever done any business with a bank. You want to have a bank account to store your money in, you need to pay fees. You need to use or withdraw your money, you need to pay fees. You want to send funds to someone else, you pay bank fees. The list goes on and on. But with Bitcoin, you're bypassing all these fees. Digital wallets are free, and transaction fees are very, very minimal.

WHY YOUR BUSINESS NEEDS TO START ACCEPTING BITCOIN PAYMENTS NOW

While many businesses have already joined the Bitcoin revolution by accepting bitcoin payments, many are still hesitant to make the jump. They are afraid that with Bitcoin's volatility, they may end up essentially giving their products or services for free. What this means is that they think they are going to get shortchanged if the price in bitcoin drops and would, therefore, lose all their profits. But this is absolutely not the case! In this article, you'll find out exactly why you shouldn't miss out on accepting bitcoin payments.

1 – INSTANT BITCOIN CONVERSION TO YOUR LOCAL CURRENCY

Bitcoin's volatility is a business owner's biggest concern. But with payment gateways like BitPay and Coinbase, you can easily bypass Bitcoin's volatility. These services will instantly convert your bitcoin payments into your local currency which you'll receive in your bank account the following business day. This means that if your customer paid you $100 worth of bitcoins, then you're going to get exactly $100 in your bank account.

2 - NO CHARGEBACKS. EVER.

One of the most common things business owners hate with credit card payments is the very real threat of receiving a chargeback. Some customers are just fickle-minded and dishonest. They would file chargebacks for the smallest reasons like they're not happy with the color they got, or they regretted the purchase, or something similar. But with bitcoin payments, you don't need to worry about chargebacks because all bitcoin transactions, once verified by the Bitcoin network, are final and irreversible. This means those bitcoins you've received are yours (unless of course, you chose to have them instantly converted to dollars).

3 - NO COSTLY PROCESSING FEES

Credit cards are widely accepted worldwide, and merchants like receiving payments from anyone with a valid card. While credit cards are convenient, there are fees that merchants need to pay. Credit card fees can range anywhere from 3% to 4% per transaction plus another few cents for each transaction made. If you receive card payments from 99% of your customers, you're basically paying a small fortune in credit card fees!

With bitcoin payments, the transaction fees you have to pay are nowhere near what you pay the credit card companies. In fact, the fees are practically negligible as they essentially come down to just a few thousand Satoshis (1 Satoshi = 0.00000001 bitcoin) or a few cents!

RED FLAGS OF CRYPTOCURRENCY SCAMS

There are many different kinds of cryptocurrency scams that are victimizing people who are new to the crypto world. Con artists prey on those who don't know the difference between a legit crypto platform and a fake one, who don't know a Ponzi scheme from a legitimate affiliate program. These scammers fool people into thinking that their well-designed websites give them a semblance of legitimacy, but on closer inspection, these sites won't pass muster. Here are some giant red flags you should be aware of:

1 - WEBSITE HAS NO SSL CERTIFI-CATE

It's very important for a website that deals with crypto-currencies to have an SSL (Secure Sockets Layer) certificate installed. Websites with no SSL only display HTTP before their domain names and websites with SSL show HTTPS. Many scam websites are here today, gone tomorrow types of sites, which means once they've scammed a certain number of people, they'll shut down that site and move on to a fresh domain. It's quite easy to transfer website files from one domain to another; this is why these scammers can set up shop very quickly.

2 – THE OFFER IS TOO GOOD TO BE TRUE

Whether you're trying to get the best rates for your dollars or bitcoins, it's only natural that you'd want the best possible deal. Since cryptocurrencies are decentralized, most crypto exchanges have their own exchange rates. However, these rates don't vary by much. If you see a website offering rates that are significantly lower or higher than other established exchanges, then it's a giant red flag. It's better to do business with a trusted platform with higher fees than to try to get the best deal out of an unknown website that could possibly swindle you out of your entire fortune.

3 - BEWARE OF PONZI SCAMS

Some Ponzi scams are not as obvious especially if they've been around for a few weeks or months. This is because their first members would already have received their profits (derived from payments by new recruits) and would be posting glowing reviews on the Internet. At first glance, you might be fooled into thinking it's a legitimate crypto operation especially if you personally know someone who's made money from the scheme. Check out those positive reviews, and you'll see they're basically saying the same thing. We'd even like to bet they would have their affiliate or referral links somewhere on the review.

BITCOIN MAIN FACTS : THE MOST INTERESTING BITCOIN FACTS EVERY BITCOIN OWNER SHOULD KNOW

BITCOIN BACKGROUND

- First successful cryptocurrency
- Originally meant to be a peer-to-peer payment system
- Addressed the problem of double spending
- Founder: Satoshi Nakamoto (pseudonym)

- Year Invented: 2008
- Technology Used: The Blockchain
- 1 bitcoin = 100,000,000 Satoshis

- Only 21,000,000 bitcoins will ever be created
- No actual intrinsic value
- Only took 5 years to breach $1000 mark

ADVANTAGES OF BITCOIN

- Very fast payments
- Very low transaction fees
- Can pay or receive bitcoins anytime of day
- Don't need a bank account

- Decentralized, open-source, transparent
- No banks or government controls it
- Not subject to politics and corruption

- Anyone can create a bitcoin wallet
- You have total control of your bitcoins

- Protects users from identity theft
- Transactions are irreversible once verified by network
- No threat of chargebacks

DISADVANTAGES OF BITCOIN

- Extremely risky
- High volatility
- Still relatively new
- Not fully matured and developed

WHAT YOU CAN BUY WITH BIT-COINS

- Common household items
- Gift cards
- Video games
- High-tech gadgets

- Plane tickets
- Rent vehicles
- Pizza, burgers, sandwiches, etc.

- Coffee, beer, etc.
- Donate to charity
- Reddit gold

- Many more items!

METHODS TO ACQUIRE BITCOIN

Buy bitcoins

- Fastest method of getting bitcoins

- Will need to spend fiat money

- Top cryptocurrency exchange / brokers:
  - Coinbase/GDAX
  - Kraken
  - Gemini o Bitstamp o CEX.io

- Cash exchanges o LocalBitcoins o Wall of Coins
- Trade other cryptocurrencies for bitcoin
  - Great if you already have other crypto

  - Don't need to spend fiat money

  - Crypto to crypto exchange
    - ShapeShift

- Get paid with bitcoins
  - Work for bitcoins

  - Sell products or services
  - Receive tips from customers

  - Complete small tasks on websites, such as:

- Complete surveys
- Watch videos
- Click ads
- Answer questions
- Sign up for trial offers
- Download mobile apps
- Play online games
- Shop online
- Join bitcoin faucets
- Get a few Satoshis at regular intervals

- Mine your own bitcoins

BITCOIN MINING

- Role of miners
  - Verifies transactions
  - Create new bitcoins
  - Without miners, there will be no new bitcoins

BITCOIN MINING TERMINOLOGY

- Blocks
- Bitcoins per block / reward
- Bitcoin difficulty

- Electricity rate
- Hash
- Hash rate

- Pool fees
- Power consumption
- Time frame

BITCOIN MINING HARDWARE USED BY MINERS

- CPU (Computer Processing Unit)
- Used in the early days

- GPU (Graphical Processing Unit)

- More efficient than CPUs
- 50-100 times more productive than CPUs

- FPGA (Field-Programmable Gate Array)

  - More powerful than CPUs and GPUs
  - Less power hungry
- ASIC (Application-Specific Integrated Circuit)

  - Primary hardware used today
  - Used solely for mining

  - Most efficient hardware
  - Consumes less power than FPGAs

- Mining difficulty

  - Average mining time – 10 minutes
  - More miners, mining difficulty increases
- Mining rewards

- Reward is halved every 210,000 blocks
- Initial reward was 50 bitcoins
- November 28, 2012 - reward was halved to 25 bitcoins
- July 9, 2016 – reward again halved to 12.5 bitcoins
- Year 2021 – reward will drop to 6.25 bitcoins

- Mining pools
  - Allow miners to pool resources
  - Divide bitcoin reward among themselves

- Cloud mining
  - No need to buy own hardware
  - No need to worry about electric bills o Pay a subscription fee start mining o Very few legit cloud mining sites
  - Most are Ponzi-style scams

BITCOIN WALLETS

- Hot wallets
  - Easy and free
  - Can be hacked
  - Can be accessed anywhere with Internet
  - Private keys are stored online
  - Example hot wallets
    - Online wallets from crypto exchanges
    - Mobile app wallets
    - Desktop wallets

- Cold wallets
  - Very difficult to hack
  - Offline storage
  - Much safer than hot wallets
  - Example cold wallets
    - Paper wallets
    - Hardware wallets

COMMON BITCOIN SCAMS

- Fake bitcoin exchanges
  - Offers too good to be true exchange rates
  - Unknown in the industry
- Phishing scams
  - Email phishing scams
  - Malware scams
- Ponzi scams
  - Offers outlandish ROI
  - Usually guarantees daily profits forever
- Cloud mining scams

TRADING VS INVESTING

- Trading is short-term
    - Takes advantage of volatility o Buy low and sell high method o Very risky
- Investing is long-term
    - Buy and hold method
    - Dollar cost averaging method

FUTURE OF CRYPTOCURRENCY

- Blockchain technology will become mainstream
- Combat crime and corruption
- Massive adoption in developing economies

BITCOIN FAMOUS QUOTES

- Cryptocurrency is such a powerful concept that it can almost overturn governments - Charles Lee

- Bitcoin will do to banks what email did to the postal industry - Rick Falkvinge

- So bitcoin is cyber snob currency - William Shatner

- Bitcoin is a technological tour de force - Bill Gates

- Bitcoin is gold for nerds - Stephen Colbert

- What can't kill Bitcoin, makes it (us) stronger - Mark Wittkowski

- The swarm is headed towards us - Satoshi Nakamoto

- It's money 2.0, a huge huge huge deal - Chamath Palihapitiya

- Bitcoin may be the TCP/IP of money - Paul Buchheit

- "Bitcoin is Cash with Wings" - Charlie Shrem

7 TECHNIQUES TO SUCCESSFUL CRYPTOCURRENCY TRADING

With the skyrocketing prices of Bitcoin, Ethereum, Litecoin, and other cryptocurrencies, more and more people are looking into cryptocurrency trading to make quick profits. The crypto market is highly volatile, with steep price jumps in a matter of minutes, and smart traders are capitalizing on this volatility. Now before we go into the seven techniques to succeed in cryptocurrency trading, let's discuss first the basics of trading, and if this is something you'd like to get into.

TRADING VS. INVESTING IN CRYP-TOCURRENCIES

These two terms are used interchangeably by many people, but they are two different strategies altogether. For one, trading is for people who want to capitalize on short-term volatility. This means they do a lot of technical analysis to determine when they should buy and sell their cryptocurrencies. These are individuals who know how to time the markets, so to speak. Doing this will require a lot of technical know-how.

Otherwise, if you jump into trading cryptocurrency blindly, then you could literally be throwing money down the drain. If you don't know what you're doing, you could lose everything. With investing, you don't worry about timing the market. You look towards the future and don't bother looking at the daily or weekly charts. Seeing near-term price dips don't bother you because you're not planning on cashing out your investment soon.

While there is a possibility that in the future when you're ready to sell your cryptocurrency and trade it for cash, the price might not be as high compared to if you liquidate your investment at the 'right time.' That's just one of the risks you'd have to take. But think about how many mini-heart attacks you're saving yourself from simply because you don't let yourself think about daily or weekly price dips!

Now that you know the pros and cons of trading and investing in cryptocurrency, let's proceed to the seven strategies for successful crypto trading:

TECHNIQUE 1 - BUY LOW AND SELL HIGH

Trading is all about making a quick buck. It is only natural that you buy crypto at low prices and then sell when the price goes up. In fact, this is why this is the top tip in this short report. Plain and simple, buying low and selling high is, for all purposes, common sense. The difference between your buying and selling price is your profit.

Now, imagine if you do the opposite. If you buy low, and you sell it at an even lower price. Think you're making a profit? Obviously, not. You'll be getting the short end of the stick. Rinsing and repeating this strategy can very quickly get you from zero to hero in a matter of days or weeks!

On the surface, this strategy might seem very simple. But executing it is actually much more difficult. Because of the volatile nature of cryptocurrencies, we don't really know if the price we're buying at is low enough.

Neither do we know if the price we're selling at is high enough. As they say, hindsight is 20/20. But if you follow the other techniques in this report, then you should be able to at least have an idea of whether the price is going to go up or down.

TECHNIQUE 2 – PAY ATTENTION TO THE NEWS

Listening to what's happening in the cryptocurrency world is easier said than done, especially if you only have a passing interest in the technical details of how cryptocurrency works. You just want to profit – that's why you're trading. You don't need to know the news, you tell yourself. Having this kind of mentality is not the right way to succeed in crypto trading. You know why?

Because cryptocurrency is not the most stable currency or commodity in the world, it's not even centralized. With no government, banks or any other central figure backing cryptocurrencies, their value is at the mercy of people who own and have access to them.

Remember that cryptocurrencies are all digital in nature, they don't have physical properties, and as such, have no intrinsic value. So its value is pretty much subject to how much the crypto community thinks it is worth.

So if something good happens in the crypto world, the price would appreciate because more people would be buying crypto. But if something bad happens, people tend to get scared easily and would sell off their digital coins in a hurry. With cryptocurrency being so new, people are skittish about putting too much faith in their digital coins.

To succeed as a crypto trader, you need to put your ear to the ground and listen close. Have a feel for what's going to happen. Is there breaking news? Is it good or bad? How do you think it's going to affect the price? When you know the answer to these questions, then you're one step closer to succeeding in trading cryptocurrencies.

TECHNIQUE 3 – LEARN TO READ CHARTS

We're not going to go into the technical details here, don't worry. It's going to take much more than a short report to cover even the basics of technical analysis. But to give you an idea, you'll need to read up, and master, popular technical analysis methods such as Japanese Candlesticks, Elliott Wave Analysis, Fibonacci Levels, Stochastics and Relative Strength Index (RSI), MACD or Moving Average Convergence / Divergence, and Ichimoku Clouds.

If you want to be a trader, you have to think like a trader. Professional traders technically live on charts because that's how they figure out whether the price is going to go up or down. Of course, they're also aware of the other techniques on this list, but most of these other methods don't really deal with math. When logic and math are applied together, you can be infinitely successful in crypto trading!

TECHNIQUE 4 – OPEN A DEMO TRADING ACCOUNT

This is a very important technique if you want to master trading cryptocurrencies someday. No one gets to run without learning how to walk first – this principle also applies to crypto trading. Practicing on a demo account is like taking small, baby steps.

It will give you a safe environment to play in so you can experience the thrill of winning or profiting. When you experience losing some demo crypto, it will teach you to be cautious. Losing will also teach you a very valuable lesson in trading – don't spend what you can't afford to lose.

With a demo trading account, you'll be able to practice how to time the market so you can buy low and sell high. You can also practice how to do technical analysis and read the crypto exchange charts. Just keep in mind that when trading in a demo environment, you have to think like you're trading in the real world.

Don't take the demo account for granted because you're not going to learn anything. If you think like it's a real account with your real money in it, you'll learn faster because you'll be hypersensitive to what you're doing and what you could be doing wrong.

It's okay to make mistakes the first few times you practice, but as time goes on, and you learn from your losses, your self-confidence should grow that you can finally leave the demo environment behind and wade in the exciting world of cryptocurrency trading!

TECHNIQUE 5 - TRADE ONLY WHAT YOU CAN AFFORD TO LOSE

You can lose all the demo money or demo crypto in your account, and you probably won't feel a thing. But when you're dealing with real money that you've worked hard for, then it's a different story.

Trading is a bit like gambling, but with trading you're supposed to take calculated risks, meaning you can use past data and current events to try to predict what's going to happen next. With real money at stake, it's even more important to learn technical analysis and pay attention to the news, so you don't lose too much, if at all. In fact, it's preferable you don't lose at all. But with the volatility of cryptocurrency, no one can really predict anything, so the best, and most sensible, thing you can do is trade only what you can afford to lose.

Once you have graduated from your demo trading account, you can start investing real money in *small amounts* . Don't try to invest huge sums right away, unless you really have a lot of spare cash to burn. You might not get huge profits when trading small amounts, but the bright side is it's also not going to hurt terribly when you lose.

And when trading, you should always brace yourself to lose out on some trades from time to time. It's just the nature of the game.

TECHNIQUE 6 – HAVE A SOLID PLAN IN PLACE

Not having a solid plan in place before you enter the world of crypto trading is like walking blind into a busy street intersection. You could get crippled, maimed, or killed instantly. Trading cryptocurrencies is not something anyone can do. It takes a special kind of discipline and intelligence for a trader to succeed. You could get lucky, but there's about a one in a billion chance of that happening.

The truth is trading cryptocurrencies is even more difficult and more challenging than trading stocks. Yes, it can be infinitely more rewarding, but the risk is also tenfold or maybe even a hundred-fold. If you think you can stomach that kind of risk, then you're welcome to try your hand at this game. Otherwise, you might be better off investing in more stable profit-generating activities.

Having a solid plan in place means you should already know beforehand at what price you should be buying and what price you should be selling. When your favorite crypto hits your set price, don't wait for it to go any higher or lower. Instead, stick to what you've planned. Getting greedy is not going to get you far. In fact, it could leave you worse off than when you started.

There will always be 'what ifs' in trading – whether it's cryptocurrency, stocks, or whatever – and like we've mentioned earlier, hindsight is always 20/20. So there's no point kicking yourself if you bought a little too early or sold a little too late. Your plan is the only thing that's stable and it will hold you steady in times of crypto volatility.

TECHNIQUE 7 – BE PREPARED FOR VOLATILITY

It's a given that all cryptocurrencies are highly volatile. No one can predict which direction the price is going to move in. Take, for example, Bitcoin. Many said its value would never surpass $1,000, but it did precisely that five years after it was first launched to the public by its founder, Satoshi Nakamoto. Now here we are just a few short years later, and Bitcoin's value is rocking the charts.

Bitcoin's skyrocketing prices are creating millionaires left and right, and this exponential growth is attracting all sorts of characters to try and take advantage of this digital gold rush. We've got ordinary people looking to get 'lucky' with Bitcoin, some smart investors looking to see if they can multiply their millions, and let's not forget the thieves, scammers, and hackers who are looking to get those precious bitcoins free of charge courtesy of their victims.

The point is that when trading or investing in cryptocurrency, you can either strike it rich or go bankrupt. Being prepared for either scenario would help a lot, but it's not going to be easy. You'd need to toughen up mentally. You'd need to simply be prepared for whatever may happen and hope for the best.

FINAL WORDS

When you combine all seven techniques, the probability of succeeding as a cryptocurrency trader is going to be much higher than if you only pick a few. With discipline, knowledge, and experience, you can easily take advantage of cryptocurrencies' volatility regularly. Before you know it, you'll be making huge gains, and your crypto portfolio will be impressing not just yourself, but the people around you too!

BITCOIN MAIN RESOURCE

We'll be honest. Bitcoin and cryptocurrencies have a very steep learning curve. It's not something that can be learned in a day unless you already have a passing interest in cryptography and cryptocurrencies in general. To a total beginner, learning how Bitcoin works is like walking in a giant maze. There are too many complicated and highly technical parts involved. This is why we've prepared this resource cheat sheet for you,so you don't get lost in the exciting and complex world of cryptocurrencies.

WEBSITES

Bitcoin.org

htt p s : / /b i tco i n.org

This site outlines the basics of Bitcoin, the features and benefits for individuals, businesses, and developers. You can read thedetailed documentationon all things Bitcoin, such as how the blockchain works, transactions, contracts, wallets, mining, and more. It has links to popular Bitcoin communities, social networks, meetups, and nonprofit organizations in many countries. If you want to see the blockchain in action, you can download the Bitcoin Core client here.

BlockGeeks

htt p s : / /bl o c k gee ks. co m /

BlockGeeks provide plenty of free, comprehensive guides about bitcoins, the blockchain,andother cryptocurrencies. If you want more, however, such as access to high-quality videos from various experts, interactive tools, and community support, then you'd need to sign up to one of their monthly subscription plans.

COURSES

The Complete Bitcoin Course

htt p s : / / ww w .udem y .co m /b i t coi n - for-be g in-ner s /

RavinderDeol's Bitcoin course is one of the most comprehensive courses on Udemy for Bitcoin. It has been reviewed by over 1,000 students with an average rating of 4.4. To date, more than 11,500 students have signed up for the course. The course is perfect for absolute beginners as well as those with a working knowledge of Bitcoin but needs more guidance. As anincentive for signing up to this paid course, he sends 0.0001 bitcoin to his students' wallets so they can experience the joys of owning real bitcoin!

Cryptoversity

<u>htt p s : / / ww w .cr y pto v ers i t y .com</u>

Chris Coney's Bitcoin and cryptocurrency courses are aimed at those who want to learn everything there is to know about modern digital currencies. The site's mission is to educate people to tap into the opportunities offered by cryptocurrencies and blockchain technology. Enrolment options include paying for each course or signing up as a patron where you pay a monthly fee to support the free podcast ('supporter' plan) as well as get access to all courses ('advocate' and 'champion' subscriptions).

COMMUNITIES

BitcoinTalk

htt p s : / /b i tco i nta l k .o r g/

BitcoinTalk is the first and largest Bitcoin forum. Satoshi Nakamoto himself made hundreds of posts on this forum between 2009 and 2010. Today, there are over 26 million posts in over 878,000 topics made by

1.4 million members. Members do not only talk about bitcoins and bitcoin mining, but they also talk about other cryptocurrencies,and there are many country-specific sub-communities as well.

BITCOIN SUBREDDIT

htt p s : / / ww w .reddit .c o m /r/B i t coi n /

This subreddit is a great starting place for people loo-king to know more about bitcoins. The Sticky FAQ should be your first stop as it's where the moderators have put together a comprehensive guide on all things bitcoin. You'll learn the very basics of Bitcoin, its key properties, where to buy and spend, how to secure your bitcoins, and even bitcoin mining. Best of all, the infor-mation is free.

Bitcoin Magazine

htt p s : / /b i tco i n m ag a zin e .com

Established in 2012, Bitcoin Magazine is one of the most established sources of up-to-date information on Bitcoin, the blockchain, and the cryptocurrency industry. In addition to publishing news articles, the site also displays live exchange rates for Bitcoin, Ethereum, Bitcoin Cash, Litecoin, Monero, and more. It also has beginner-friendly guides on how Bitcoin works.

BOOKS

"Digital Gold" by Nathaniel Popper

htt p s : / / ww w .a m azon.co m / D igi t a l - Gold - Bi t coin- M illiona i re s - R ein v ent/dp/0062 3 625 0 X

Written by New York Times reporter, Daniel Popper, this book is journalism at its finest. If you want to learn about how Bitcoin began and know more about the major characters in its history, then you need to read this book. After reading this, you'll have a deep understanding of the Bitcoin subculture and how it will affect the global financial market.

" Th e A g e Of C r y p t o cu rre n c y " b y M i c h ael J . C as e y a n d Pa u l V i gn a htt p s : / / ww w .a m azon.co m /Ag e - C r y pto c urrenc y -Blo c k c hai n - C hallengin g - Econo m i c/ d p/12 50 081556

Written by seasoned reporters, this book seeks to answer the question, "Why should you care about Bitcoin?" The authors will walk you through the history of Bitcoin, the blockchain, and cryptocurrency in general. It also provides a broad overview and analysis of the future of cryptocurrency as well as how it relates to the world economic system.

"Mastering Bitcoin" by Andreas M. Antonopoulos

htt p s : / / ww w .a m azon.co m / M a s teri n g -B i tco i n - U nlo c kin g - D igital- C r y ptocurrenci e s / d p/1449374 042

Authored by one of the most well-known Bitcoin evangelists today, this book will help coders and those technically inclined to understand how Bitcoin really works, the technology behind it (the blockchain), and how it can be applied in the real world. For those interested in bitcoin mining, this book has an entire section dedicated to this topic.

VIDEOS

Crypto Bobby's YouTube Channel

htt p s : / / ww w . y outube. c o m / channe l / UCt_o M 56 U i0B CC gi0Y c - W h3Q

If you want daily updates and opinions on the latest happenings in the cryptocurrency world, you should sub-scribe to this guy's channel. He doesn't advertise himself as an expert, rather he's just sharing his honest thoughts on Bitcoin, Ethereum, Litecoin, and any of the other ra-pidly growing cryptocurrencies.

Bitcoin.com's YouTube Channel

htt p s : / / ww w . y outube. c o m / channe l / UC et x k Z olEB H X 4 7 Bq tZ kt b kg/

Bitcoin.com's channel is full of exciting videos on everything Bitcoin related. They have videos on the basics of how this cryptocurrency works as well as news of what's happening in the Bitcoin world. Their website is also a great place to start if you want to know more about bitcoins – you can even sign up for a free 10-day email course.

PODCASTS

The Bitcoin Podcast

htt p s : / /t h ebi t coin po dc a s t .co m /

With over 170 episodes aired so far, the Bitcoin podcast is one of the original podcasts in the cryptocurrency world. It has a set of regular hosts,and they interview guests regularly, most of whom are instructors, producers, and writers in the crypto community. They air a new episode every week with each one running around 60-80 minutes or so.

BITCOIN KNOWLEDGE

<u>htt p : // w w w .bitcoin .k n/</u>

In this podcast, Trace Mayer, one of the leading experts in Bitcoin, interviews top people in the Bitcoin, blockchain,andfintech (financial technology) space. They discuss a wide variety of topics, from the technical to investments to business functions. If you're interested in finding out how blockchain technology is being implemented in the real world, then subscribe to this podcast.

www.ingramcontent.com/pod-product-compliance
Lightning Source LLC
Chambersburg PA
CBHW061148180526
45170CB00002B/671